Between Me and My Bones

poems for the perseverant heart

Kailey Murphy

Written by Kailey Murphy

Cover Art by Brooke Sunderland

Cover Design by Brooke Sunderland & Kailey Murphy

Inquiries can be directed to kailey@moonbodyliving.com

Please visit www.moonbodyliving.com for more information.

For anyone who longs for liberation
in the bruised and beautiful world,
this is for you.

For my family and friends,
who have given me love in every color,
I bow to you.

Contents

Introduction

These are the poems
inside my palms,
carved from a moon
waxing into wonder,
pulsing from a body
drenched in stars.

As I write to you now, I am in the final year of my 20s — a decade of my life that has felt like a messy, wild, magnificent unfolding in search of myself. During this time, my body traversed many landscapes from New York to Kauai to Colorado and Greece, but it is the inner journey that I am most drawn in by: the hills and valleys, oceans and forests that live and breathe in the spaces between my bones.

This internal landscape has been one of pain, addiction, love and loss, where, at times, I have felt trapped by my body and a feeling of brokenness, where I have longed for every ache to heal so that I may sing in bliss.

But underneath it all was this wise one — a voice that came to me most intimately through poetry as words unspooled from my soul and I awakened to a haven that lives within each moment, if only I pause and listen.

These poems are in devotion to both our humanness and our divinity — this seemingly paradoxical relationship between being born into form and yet being a part of something eternally formless. For me, the magic exists not in casting out my humanness but in welcoming it all: the mess and the magnificence, the ache and the awakening, the body and the beloved.

And so I offer these poems to you with a soft heart in the hope that they may touch the places within you that yearn for love and tenderness. That in reading snippets from my soul, you may begin to discover the boundlessness that comes from the breaking and the remembrance that reemerges as we stop running and start feeling. So that together we may soften into all the spaces inside, embodying a love so vast it makes the whole world dance.

Between Me and My Bones

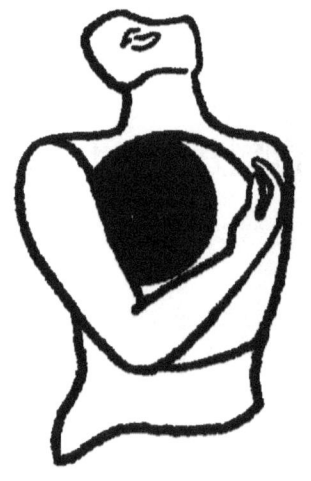

ONE DAY

Sometimes when the swans
make love on the languid lake
and the silty river swallows
the sky from my mouth,
I sit and wonder,

if I search beneath all the leaves,
will I find the one you dangle upon,
bundled in your cocoon,
swaying as a chandelier
in a house of cedar and pine?

And if I touch you with my fingers,
will you shiver and then shatter
or shall you remain
in a nest of tarantula trees
dressed in mossy desire?

Waning into shadow,
the moon smiles
at those who dare to wander
while most are in slumber.

Wouldn't you like to see her,
fly to her if you may,
greet her with your wings
like a blue flame in the night?

For today,
I stood beneath
the arms of a tree,
bristled gray, as if to say,
I, too, shall die.

For it is this truth —
the only truth —
we seem to forget
while suffocating
in our silk casings,
thinking, perhaps one day,
we will fly.

Part One:

HUNGER

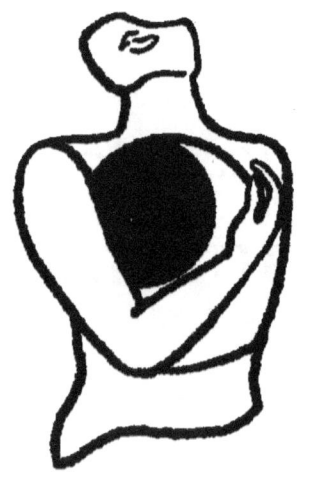

THE UNTETHERED

If my wings unfurled
and I could see the world
as a billowing cloud
on the brink of rain,
your scent would still
intoxicate my inhales,
your shadow still haunting
the hallway of my dreams,
your back still resting
on the chair at my table.
And I would ask for forgiveness
as if the giving of that gift
would loosen the knots
in my braided bones,
as if the hearing of your voice
would unbound my heart.
And when I rise,
I'd rise with remembrance
and when I dance,
I'd dance with the dawn.
For in those soundless hours,
it is not the longing for bliss

nor the sweet relief of

pleasure's pithy tongue

that molests my mind

but the aching of the tethered,

the formless wrapped in form,

wailing,

when shall we be free?

IN AUTUMN

I've written many a poem
where I speak of the blushed leaves,
of the burgundy and golden hues
falling like snow in the distance,
how they pirouette in the air,
spinning in bliss like the Sufi mystics.

And the branches do not bleed,
do not shriek or shrivel in their nakedness
but embrace the anointing of the first flake,
of which they wear like a silvery dress.

And I wonder if this is true for me too:
if I may fall as gracefully as the leaves?

For these days, I find my hands in fists —
my jaw clenched for catastrophe,
waking to sirens in the streams of my psyche.
And I carry the terror in the twist of my tongue,
the words sticking like sap to my skin.
All the many ways I belittle and berate
and sedate myself,

I fight for them to fall away.

For these days, I yearn
for the silent stroke of lightning
to slap me out of sleepiness,
so sudden and electric,
it burns all the filth into flames.

But what is to be said of the solitary leaf
that travels from branch to earth body,
without question or command,
just because,
just because.

ON ADDICTION: PART 1

Tiredness tugs at me

like an incessant child,

reminding me of the choices I've made

to get to a place of such weariness.

I wish to doze off but

the burden of the body breathing

punctures me into paralysis.

My legs are numb;

the smoke of seduction

now infiltrating my lungs.

They tell me to rise up,

these voices in my head,

but how is a branded being

supposed to stop

all the craving and dreaming?

Not by choice nor by force —

this is what I know.

When you come inside of me,

I wish you could hear

how mighty she is —

how her voice is silky softness

and yet strong as bone and tree,

how she commandeers a ship

who never surrenders

and always shouts:

this is the way out!

And I believe.

IN THE CHURCH BASEMENT

I sit in the basement of a church
with five other women,
all of us strung together
by a common dis-ease.

My life, I am learning,
has been one great running
away from the ache.

I am reminded of this
every time I stare
at my swollen fingers
coated in food
or my eyes after
hours of isolation.

But I keep coming back
to these basements
with the blue books and
the serene women
in search of a solution.

We go around the circle
introducing ourselves,
and I wonder,
can I still be loved
if this is who I am?

As we pray,
my eyes close in to the chaos
but the hands of the holy
rest upon my heart.
Her lips — a kiss —
on the highest point
of my head.
And somewhere,
someone
turns on a light.

Years ago,
I saw my body
still in a frozen stream
as I wailed
for death's descent
inside my mind.

But here,

on this metal chair

in this musky room

with your lips,

your hands, your song

strumming inside my skin,

I remember,

it is through living,

I unearth love.

CAULDRON OF CURIOSITY

I tell you

I am frightened:

young as I am,

my body feels bound

by a brokenness

I cannot shake off.

It shivers inside,

like frozen fists of ice,

refusing to thaw.

I long for the sun,

I tell you,

to grace me

with his grandeur,

to melt the pain into puddles

so that I may play

in bare, mud-caked feet,

to be as unfettered as a child

who flings herself

into the cauldron

of curiosity,

wild in her wonder,

who forgets

all at once

she is of a dying form,

who remembers

all at once

she is a ray

of sunlit love.

ON DREAMS

I scratch at my dreams
like a dog in the dirt,
digging for bones
scattered in the backyard
of a mind, full and in pain.

A wisp of her hair and
the contours of a man,
a feeling — heaving
in its recession —
hang inside like
tattered cloth on a line.

The wind blows them
towards me and then
breathes them away
as if it is natural
to spend a third of my life
behind still eyes.

Who decides as I write
this is waking life?

Who decides
I must rest in the night?
Who is the face,
and where is her hair?

And if I search and sift
through patterns of plastic
littered inside a skull
sculpted to survive,
will I touch with humble hands
what it is I am grasping for?

I swear to you,
I do not know,
I cannot know
but only dream.

For when you sleep tonight,
will you arrange me in your world?
A world I can never breathe in,
a world I can never find —
only visit like a gust of wind,
a piece of littered plastic,
a cloth on the line.

A BUTTERFLY

She came to me,

not between my thighs

of flesh and fluid,

nor beneath my

humble hardened feet,

but rather

through the alleyway

of a torn heart,

dressed in all

her damaged delight.

And I wept at her

windowless abode as she

beckoned me within —

her roots wrapping

around my ankles,

her octopus arms

outstretched

to the loss of Eden.

Inside here,

there are no lights

casting shadow,

only the cavern of a chrysalis

frozen still by the silence.

Inside here,

I chisel at

the marbled masks

upon my face,

revealing lips

and then teeth

and then tongue,

revealing cheeks

and then bone

and then breath,

until the room begins

to glow with the

embers of my eyes,

and there she is,

this creature of pain

I have denounced

my entire life,

there she is —

a butterfly.

NEEDLE & PINE

If I could,

I'd let you rip the fabric

right out of my mind,

tear it into pieces,

and clothe the naked,

because I am not hungry

but I keep eating,

because I am not tired,

but I keep sleeping.

And I ask of you the Almighty,

am I the needle or the pine?

And if I could,

would you let me

be the breeze

or the selfless moon

in the star-drunk sky

or the indigo dye

from the elderberry bush

or the hand that gathers

or the basket that holds?

Could I be

the slithering smoke

of a just lit incense

or the liquor that lingers

on his lips

or the marigold closing

in a field of mist?

Could I be the mischievous

laughter of a child

or the lollipop in her mouth

or the blood on his knee,

streaming like a river

from his oceanic heart?

Could I be the angel

arching above their heads

or the solitary drop of water

on her tongue?

Could I be a song

or a whisper

or the silent sweep

of death itself ?

I ask of you,

could I be the needle

and the pine?

THE GIFT OF FLIGHT

I gave a slice of myself to the sky that day,
to the little rainbows of light
dusted inside sprawling clouds,
to the pockets of azure blue peeking through,
and I found my breath in that great body
where birds fly near the eyes of God
and jets stream the sphere with lines of white.
Here on earth,
gravity grips me like a lover in the night,
but just once, I ask him,
will you grant me the gift of flight?

THE RISE

Today I witnessed
the one who abandons.
She crept away, slowly now,
leaving my orphaned parts
in a bruised bassinet
until her presence was all
but a mirage in my mind.
And I wonder now,
how does she unspool the self,
and who is left widowed
when she unwinds?
Or does she continue to reside
in the cellar of my skull,
aching to be ignited?
And perhaps
it is her brazen act
of renunciation
that is her brilliance,
her complete ceasefire
of the war within
that is her holy wine,
proclaiming her nothingness

and undressing her desires

as she thrusts her body

into the fire,

burning,

and then

tenderly

rising.

ON ADDICTION: PART II

I remember how her arms

wrapped around my body,

so soft and inviting,

like a blanket or a lover

on those first mornings,

and I sought refuge on her island,

swimming in secluded waters.

Just you and me,

she whispered,

just you and me.

So I kept on returning

whenever I was hungry,

a frequent visitor

revolving around the door,

but my head became dizzy

and the waters lost their rapture,

swallowing my body

with its taunting teeth.

And I would leave each time

without a limb or a laugh,

with battered lips and bloated belly,

but I was a loyal voyager —

a faithful friend.

Until on that day,

imprisoned by impulse,

I drowned in the waves

and sank into the swirl of dark waters.

There in the sand,

a pearl glistened like a firefly

aglow in the night,

soft and inviting,

illuminating my insides

with the very substance I sought

all those years ago.

Welcome, she said,

stop searching in the sand

and let the light engulf you.

Do not wear it as a dress

to be taken on and off;

instead, let it swallow you

until you shimmer,

let it bathe your every breath

as you shine like iridescent fish scales

in the swarming sea.

For if I am to be an addict,

I shall be addicted to a soul-led life,

and if I am to swim,

it shall be in the crest
of the Creator's wave,
and if I am to rest,
it shall be in the breast
of the boundless heart.

Part Two:

HEART(ACHE)

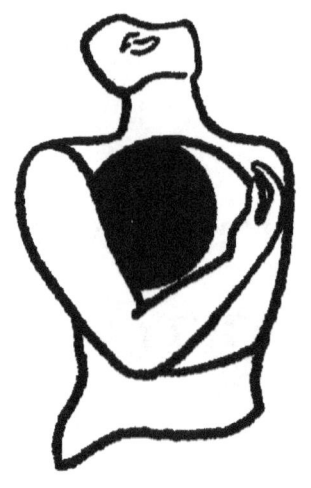

MY LOVE

There are things in my mind,

stories of which I wish

to whisper

in the soft channels

of your heart,

like dewdrops on

the slender stem

of a sleep-dusted flower,

rousing at dawn.

SWOLLEN PINK LIPS

Tonight, I unraveled
my earth-dyed fingers
to touch the weavings
of your spine until
every bone cracked
open to bliss.

And in darkness,
I kissed the freckles
on your face —
each one
a tiny sun
I wished to burn in.

Tonight we drank
the yoke of our union,
drunk on the love
that comes
from losing the self
to something sacred.

And we came,

again and again,

like thirsty visitors,

to the place that

only saints speak of.

And if for all my days

I chose only this —

to rest across

your bare back

in naked abandon

and breathe in time

until my body

was no longer mine,

I'd forever feel

the taste of God

on swollen pink lips.

THE SPACE BETWEEN

The soul burns blue
out of your well-worn mouth
as tendrils wrap around brittle wrists,
aching to be awakened.
The lines of our bodies
soften into charcoal shades
scribbled in the dark
while cracks sound out of
the latches of my spine.
This fence dividing me, dividing us,
has been broken
as you breathe into the liminal
spaces between my bones,
where secrets swim in synovial fluid
and time suspends herself
in lungs of lavender,
awaiting oxygen.
For today,
be my eyes and my breasts,
be where the fullness of life
and the absence of it meet,
be like the sea reaching towards the shore

only do not drift away —

stay.

Stay in this ecotone of existence

where the shells gather and

the rocks gleam.

For I was born out of a womb

and I will return to one,

but here,

here I am without a name

and without a spine.

In the space between,

I was never birthed

and I will never die.

LOVING INTO LOSS

The other night
two women made love in my skull,
and I woke wet with wanting.

And I remembered their bodies,
curved like quivering question marks,
their salt tears swirling in a single stew.

I remembered the sips they took
of each other's skin,
how this act was not luxury
but a necessity —
as essential as air and water.

But most of all,
I remembered the grief that grew
around the trunk of their union,
like a parasitic vine.

For every time we choose love,
we choose loss.

IN MEMORY / IN MORNING

Our corner of the world is awakening.

A blanket of clouds casts the sky in slate

but the light sparks at the edges

where blazing blue

meets effervescent white,

and I remember.

I remember loving you not so long ago

with fields of hope sprouting

a bounty of our foreboding.

And on our farewell night,

I remember the circles of suffering

underneath your eyes.

I painted them with the same light

from the blazing blue sky.

But I am not the healer of wounds

nor the painter of the heart.

And so I surrender

to the letting go of our love

for it is you who must create

the colors to paint

in your little corner

of the vast, vast world.

ON RAGE

I am angry, some of the time,

and it holds me like a snake

round the neck,

slithering me into suffocation.

And I dream, some of the time,

of a face on pavement,

bloody and bruised.

I cannot tell,

is it mine or is it yours?

And so I cry and then I eat

and then I starve and then I eat,

imagining my sacrificed self

hanging like flesh on a butcher's line.

For most of the time,

you are a character,

cast and christened,

in the ceaseless drama

scripted beneath my skull.

But the thieves always come

stealing you from my story,

but the thieves always come

arresting what is left of our glory.

And so I watch you flicker

like a flame

only to extinguish,

breathe you in

like stale air

only to relinquish

my love for you.

A PLACE WHERE NOTHING BREAKS

Years sprawled out between us,

chapters of our lives written and revised

and still, you lived on

in thought and melody,

in nights of possibility.

With you I learned

the margins of paradise

are meant to recede and decay,

that golden sunshine must burn

if skin is left out all day.

So how is it I still wonder,

still play the scenes of our life —

a merry-go-round of memories never made.

Though I look for you sometimes,

I think it best we never meet again.

Best the sharp shears of reality

never slash my secret scripture,

to keep me drafting dreams

I need never follow.

Best I keep us safe:

two perfect dolls making love

in a place where nothing breaks.

ON GRIEF

For there may come a time
when you fold into your grief,
like petals of a poppy
wilting at dusk.

Fall into the field, my dear,
and feel the pulse of a night living
beneath a fine-mesh sky
with stars who speak
and rocks who burn.

For in your dark hour,
children will sleep and lovers will moan,
but you will wail the midnight howl
of a house made hollow.

Do not fill the spaces.
Do not fix the door.
Leave the table un-set, floor un-swept
in all its glorious wreckage
and dissolve.

Dissolve into dirt
until your clay body crumbles
and your soul sings with the seeds,
for your tears shall baptize the birth
of a thousand buried beings

who await the glory
of the glistening sun
with every slithering root,
with every sprouting tree,

as something grows
not from nothing
but from everything
you have lost.

WATER & OIL

Downstairs in the kitchen,
I am dressed for a return to life.
Two weeks of serpents spiraling a staff,
and here, only my silhouette
is amongst the Rockies.

The image of her body
in the hospital bed is not a memory:
it is as real as the breath that ran through the tube.
And I am still in the small, cement room
with the pictures reflected on the wall.
Those photographs are the memories,
of feigned grins captured in eight by ten frames —
only the candid retain any spark in my pupils.

Samantha is perched atop her chair.
Genetically the resemblance is haunting,
not outwardly so in the color of her hair
or the formation of her figure,
but in subtle and strange ways
that make you look twice at
the movement of her index finger.

The fireflies dance along to George Harrison's sitar
and circulate hope throughout the room.
Many have been captured in jars to take home
and cradle by the firelight.
Reaching out,
I grasp the imperiled creature
and bury it in my pocket.

Mother holds sister holds friend holds lover
holds lover's mother holds neighbor
holds me holds Cynthia's
hand.

And my mind bargains with death
as a prostitute in this life
while my soul prays to the white man
with the gray beard,
because sometimes when you are desperate
and afraid, you act in ways
you no longer believe in.

The laptop keeps playing,
as the record once did,
the songs that are no longer songs
but are just Cynthia.

And the pocket is now empty.

The words of the poem
on the lawn in Tennessee
pierce my eardrums,
"Dreamy firefly wonder of a sky,
aren't you right there?"

And I find that I am neither here nor there —
not in the room with the picture frames
nor on the grass in Tennessee.
I am in the Rockies,
in the kitchen in the Rockies.

And the bottle is falling, slowly now,
onto the floor. The once whole structure
shattering into deviating sections,
and I am falling, slowly now,
onto the floor after it
with knees of crimson and
shadowy tights of greasy stains,
peering through saturated eyes
at the water and oil,
refusing to mix.

WINGED SEEDS

And still, I have not forgotten the rain

gathered on the window like stars

on nights when God was honey and wine.

And I remembered, all at once,

the fireflies circling inside

a hospital room —

creatures with a pulse

that shimmer and fade

then shimmer again.

I buried them, these winged seeds,

in places where little shines,

in spaces where grief grows.

But today, the wind carried with it

the whisper of your name

and the song on the stereo

was a sliver of ours

from the grass in Tennessee

before the accident and the ache.

Something in the way she moves,

Paul sang to us between

ukulele strums and star-dusted rain

as we merged into a moment,

as we met a kind of euphoric death

before you were gone,

as the fireflies, these winged seeds,

blossomed and breathed all around,

teaching us how it is to be free.

GOLDEN ACHE

When she comes, do not resist:

be like the field who welcomes the rain

or the hawk who does not hide

but glides with the wind.

Undress yourself in the shadows

and then sit in the splintering night —

naked and willing to burn.

What is asked of you is not easy

and yet, dear one,

there is gold in the ache.

BEYOND

There is a place beyond the pain —
I shall meet you there.
Not when the flowers bloom
or the sun shimmers,
but when every last tear has fallen
and there you lie
fetal on the floor,
excavating every ancient ache.
For when you have known the darkness
as a child knows her mother's womb,
and you have walked with sorrow
until you were swallowed,
then — and only then —
will you find this place
that was never lost
but deeply buried
in the stories you kept silent,
in the breath you held hostage,
in the heart that once hurt
and is now whole.

AT HER ALTAR

I will not lie nor
douse the self in light
when darkness draws near;
rather, I will cast my arms
as wide as the ocean
and let everything swim.
I will suffer beside the self
so as to know compassion
and the oneness of things.
I will bow to the fractured parts,
giving praise to she who
brings forth the night.
Intimately now,
almost entwined,
though still a breath apart,
I am breaking and becoming
at her altar.

Part Three:

HEALING

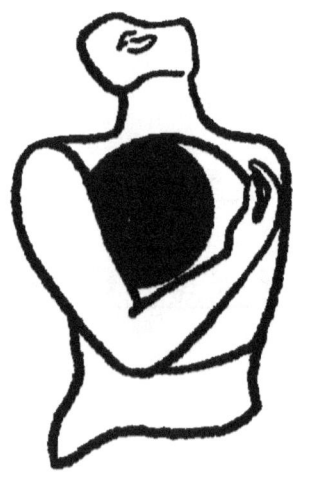

IN LOVE / IN LONGING

Sitting across from love,

I saw my eyes

reflected in every

ruinous thing,

but, for once,

I did not run from

the destruction.

And I found,

these, too, were

sewn with sanctity —

this ache and

this wound and

this hurting body —

because they brought me

here to you.

Sitting across from love,

I was at once not afraid

of the loss that comes

from loving but of

the death that comes from

anesthetic living.

And so I unfurled
my fists to feel
the wind kissing
each and every finger,
and I wept for the feeling.

Sitting across from love,
I learned the language
of listening and the necessity
of receiving.
I felt the sigh of grace
exhaling from my
own two lungs,
spreading to those
who need it.
And I saw where
we come from
and where we go
and how the two
are just the same.

Sitting across from love,
I felt my belly
birthed by love,
my pain

imbued with love,

my feet

falling in love

with the earth's blood

beneath me.

And I felt an intimacy

with the passing rain

and the early morning mist,

a closeness to what came

before my name

was written.

Sitting across from love,

I found I am often

not in love,

I am in longing.

Even now

as I write this,

in longing

for something

to be different.

Even now,

in longing

for you.

IN OUR SHATTERING

In our shattering,

I remembered

how to dance,

how to move

my hips

to the rhythm

of my rapture

and cleanse in

the tears

of my unweaving.

And I remembered

how to hold

the seams of

my suffering,

braiding them

into a quilt

of utter kindness,

how to feel

the etchings

of eternal love

in the sidewalks

of my psyche
where laughter lives
like a child
playing hopscotch
and silence
is a sound
I listen to
like music.

In our shattering,
I remembered
the enchantment
of my blood
and the euphoria
of my thighs,
the pools
of passion
swimming in
my irises,
the nameless one
who never dies.

In our shattering,
I remembered
how it is

to yearn

for not

what is good

but what

is tender,

to recover

all that has been

ransacked

and to relish myself

in reverence.

In our shattering,

I remembered

what it means

to be

unbound

in my brokenness,

magnificent

in my mourning.

NEW YEAR

Another year turned as I masqueraded joy
with gin on the tongue in the electric white city,
and I traveled home to the Rockies
knowing it would be the last time
for a long time.

I presumed my dreams
would guide me where to go,
but it was the ache in my throat
that spoke to me:
there is no other way but back,

back towards the eastern sun
rising as mama and I ventured
along the highways to New York —
the loss of a half-lived life
still lingering on my lips.

The dawn of spring came and with it a lesson:
the reward for acts of courage
is not always presented
as you wish it to be.

Swallows sought refuge in the sinews of my soul,

and though I begged for them to sing,

I heard a different voice.

Growing intimate with stories,

only read in solitude,

the cascade of song to speech to silence

saturated my every bone.

In the hills of the Hudson,

I discovered my eyes

are still the same color,

and I came to befriend myself,

to greet each day as a gift,

to breathe before eating,

to love someone and let go.

Another year turns in the city,

the white sky is on frozen ground

and I speak with the swallows,

the sight of the rising sun

no longer blinding,

the conditions of my body

no longer a limit to my joy.

In a sober ceremony,

a candle burns between generations

as an act of courage awaits me.

My feet venture westward

to the house of prayer

on the garden isle

where I come to find

the home of the holy

is but only inside.

FOR YOU, DEAR SHADOW

For so long,
I wanted to overcome —
to rise above
the rupture that happened
so many years ago
between food and form,
to stand above
with the stamp of success
stitched into my smile,
knowing I have fought it
and I have won.

But when I reach into
the recesses of my remembrance
and hold the heart of this pattern,
I do not discover destruction
but rather a love —
aching to be acknowledged —
and a girl, who knew not her power
but her pain (so near,
she sliced it into her own skin).

And now, amongst all my striving,

she asks of me only this:

is there space for me?

Perhaps after all these years

of battling, of fixing,

of extinguishing the part

I most deemed damaged,

I am here simply to make space.

To open to the one

who reaches for food

in the ways I now reach for Spirit —

gentle, soft, and slow.

To weave what has been silenced

into my wise body and make it song

where every instrument creates a sound.

For in that sound is a symphony,

so stunning,

it is the whole of me.

INVISIBLE ILLNESS

It began in the space where I once sang
and then spread slowly, like magma
moving beneath the flesh.
Six years past and the pain rises each day like ritual,
greeting me with her sirens of sensation.
Some days the muscles clench until I begin to weep
and the aches calcify until I must rest and resign.
Some days a few simple steps can ignite a forest fire;
a few simple words can lead me to silence.
Some nights I dream of a foreign body
doing the things my body hurts to do.
I imagine her singing sweetly to the forest stream
and dancing in a pool of midnight moonlight.
Tucked inside this animating creature,
I caress the world with a forgotten freedom
I hope to reclaim in this momentary life.
For when the body rejects many a thing,
I then can reject the body,
blaming her for the ways in which
she does not fit into society's ableist frames.
Yet when I am still enough,
I find there is nowhere I would rather be

but inside this transient temple
that is briefly and miraculously mine.

TO SHINE INSIDE THE DARKNESS

It is true —
I cannot stare at the sun
as he sits on his circadian throne
like some grand, cosmic king.

But the moon,
the moon I can gaze into:
see her craters and shaded edges,
where she waxes and where she wanes.
Even at her fullest,
I can behold her ripe belly
and swelling breasts
and delight in her growing glory.

And perhaps it is the night —
this devoting darkness —
that holds her like a vast net
cast out across creation.
So that when she arrives,
as she always does,
whether as a slivering crescent
or a pregnant, shimmering coin,

he is there and he is ready

to embrace her

and her ever-changing form.

I've often heard that the light

chases away the darkness

and there are those who

rejoice in the rising,

but what of the stars,

the faraway planets and

the mysterious moon

who shine inside the darkness,

not puncturing nor casting out

but coexisting, almost yearning,

for their many loves

in the same sky.

LITTLE SEEDLING OF SURRENDER

Yesterday I went to the garden

where green life grows,

but it was not the golden tomatoes

nor the emerald curls of kale

that aroused my attention

but the soft quilt of soil

and all that lives inside her loamy womb.

For when you have descended so deeply

into the burrow of great burden,

digging with dirt-dyed fingers for a spark,

perhaps there is nothing left to be done

but to sleep beside the creatures

who crawl in the dark.

To plant your body and all her foreboding

amongst root and rhizome, protozoa and prayer

as sun and rain feed you with their care.

Until with patience and time,

radicles run like rivulets out of your spine

as you crack open, little seedling,

sprouting towards that blue sphere of sky.

WAIT, DEAR ONE

Sometimes when I write,

I am like a dog hungry for dinner,

panting through pages of other poets

looking for a kibble of inspiration.

Meanwhile, there is another

who lives inside my body,

who quivers beneath my tongue,

whispering — *wait, dear one.*

Let us be married to the mystery.

Let us not strive for anything large or small.

Let us be so surrendered

that the muse lies down upon your feet

and reveals to you the source of it all.

THE WORLD DOES NOT NEED YOUR SMILE

The world does not need your smile,

unless it is stitched with truth.

The world needs your heart, open and willing.

How does it feel to devote yourself to this —

to the great unraveling of self and deceit

until you are seated in the flame of emptiness.

The fire is full of embers now,

and the ancient oak is trying to bloom,

or is it me who tries and the tree who just…

waits

for branch and bud to kiss one another

as they co-create a vision

carved from the sinew of every creature.

Today the leaves are brushed with minty green.

Tomorrow the branches bear catkins.

How fleeting this fortress is!

And yet, I continue

to enter an earth adorned with grief,

to grieve a body adorned with love.

THE TURNING

I, too, envision an awakened world —
a world where the lungs of the earth
no longer fight to breathe,
a compassionate world, a kind world,
where love is the language
we not only speak
but sing.

But first there is the burning
of all we have collected,
of all we have consumed.
There is the fire we never wished for
but somehow needed.
There is the swelling of smoke
until we cannot see
all the structures
we once deemed worthy.

And then there is the grieving —
the ashes of people and of power,
the families without funerals,
holding hearts and holding vigil.

There are the tears buried beneath
the terror, the loss of physical touch
with one another.

And too, there is the stillness —
the ceaseless silence full of freedom
if only we sit and listen.
And there are the places
within you, within me,
grand as mountains yet
clear as the stream
of who we truly are
and what we shall be.

And I wish to say
there will come a day when
you embrace the friend
you have not seen,
so sweetly now,
as if for the first time,
cradling one another
like you are each other's mothers.

And then one morning
when all is past,

you will notice the tree
in your front lawn,
bestowing the world with
her cherry-blossomed beauty,
and you will pause,
and you will breathe,
and you will worship,
before continuing on.

OUR WOUNDS

Some wounds are not meant to be held alone.

Some wounds are stitched so deeply into skin,

we have forgotten how it is we unknit and walk again.

Some wounds are of a grandeur so glacial,

we must crack the ice with a collective cry

and weep together from one eye.

Some wounds are not bleeding but bound —

bound by still tongues who have forgotten how to sing

to one another, how to behold the beauty in another.

Some wounds are carried on our grandmothers' backs,

fed into the caverns of our mothers' mouths,

whispered into the marrow of our children's bones,

buried into spaces where only crimson flows.

Some wounds are not meant to be held by a solitary self

but cradled in the net of a billion lives,

every jewel ablaze on the Beloved's neck and spine.

Some wounds are not yours, not mine —

they are ours to bleed and to bathe,

they are ours to hold and to heal,

they are ours to praise

in time.

Part Four:

HOMECOMING

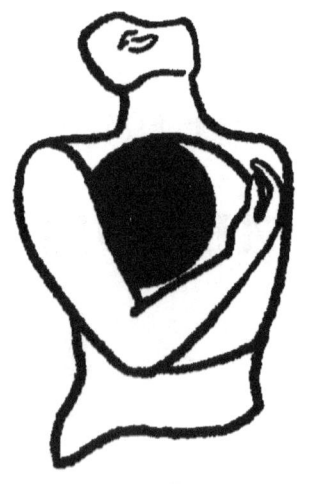

AN INVITATION

Come now,

quiet and quilted,

to the lull beyond the lunacy,

to the iris of awakened dreams.

Where shadows slither into mist,

the cascade of feelings

evaporates into nothingness.

And the red burning flame

is solely a flicker,

and the spelling of your name

is a false signature.

Where melodies cease

as the drone of dark dims

the harrowing screech

of the loneliest hawk.

Here the storm is silent.

Here the harp weeps.

For never has the blood

felt so warm.

For never has the word

heard itself to be a song.

Come now and sit

at the table

in the garden

where no one

and everyone feasts,

where nothing

and everything blooms.

MY GOD

Draw me on your easel.

Etch the lines of my hands.

For if you were to mold me

in the glow of dawn,

I'd never make love again

for that single ray of day-shine

would forever feed my fleeting skin.

AN ODE TO MY GRANDMA

There is life growing at the window,

sun streaming in at dawn,

sparrows announcing the arrival

of liminal light.

On this morning,

I hear the sounds of my grandma.

Her loud cries of laughter,

ringing from the cathedral of her body.

The way she swells so fully with joy,

she begins to shake like a leaf

on an ancient oak tree.

And her limbs reaching out to each of us

as we taste the sap of sweetness

on our own tongues.

Aunts, sisters, cousins, kin —

all stitched into a moment of unabashed glee.

Teetering on the edge of cackle and cry,

again she releases

and this time begins to weep.

A parade of tears form a river running
from her to me,
and I am drenched in a world
where only the heart speaks.

Two thousand miles apart and
I can still hear her on this morning,
still feel her in the spaces between my bones
as I crack myself open, again and again,
to boundless bliss.

CHASMS OF CREATION

I walk and the wind
makes everything sing.

The ash tree creaks like
the attic of an old home;
the tall grass rustles and speaks
like cicadas on a summer's eve.

The water in the pond,
filling with ducks and geese,
casts calm waves
onto the mud-caked shore,
where my feet wish to sink.

The sun is waving its daily goodbye
as clouds merge with shimmering rays.
And the soft hue of dusk
douses the sky
before the dominion of night.

I walk and I am taken
by a reverent euphoria,

almost in disbelief that the world
can be anything but this —
so ordinarily astounding.

I wonder, does she see it too?

The woman rushing towards me
with head turned down
and earbuds in,
or what about the man
sitting in his car,
typing on his phone,
does he feel it?

That this moment here
is what the sages speak of,
of why men go into caves
to meditate and find God.

That right here on this muddy path
is a chasm of creation,
split open by the sacred —
a little plot of the kingdom,
written and revealed.

Stop — if only for an instant —
and you shall see it too:
the bruised and beautiful world
making love to everything.

SEVEN MINUTES OF SEEING

I long to cup my hands
around the hardened clay,
clay crafted into mountains

of hushed pink and terra-cotta
trimmed with gold,
flecks of black and the curved back
of a handle bending
towards the beginning.

Here I am transfixed:
spellbound by the beauty
of a simple mug
baked inside a California kiln.

How grand that I could fall
for such a thing
just by looking deep
and even, call it love.

Seven minutes of seeing
and I now know this:

we must deepen the gaze.

We must deepen the gaze
until we become enraptured
by another's existence.

To look —
even at the one we loathe —
and notice the mountains
of hushed pink,

to behold the cracks in the clay,
remembering they, too,
can fill with gold
one day.

Offer the self to another
and steep in their mug of tea
until you and I disappear
and we see *we*.

THE UNSEEN

There is stone
who sings in her silence
and willow who waltzes
with wind.
There is slate sky clouds
holding storm
and air saturated
with nearing rain.
There is darkness
composed of star-shine
and moon
made of laughing light.
There is the voice of you,
stitched in my skull,
your lost touch
lingering on skin.
There is the heart
of my mama
beating inside mine
and the hands
of her daughter
crafting this poem.

There is the friend,

without a body,

whom I still embrace;

there is her melody serenading

every place that aches.

All my life there has been this,

a yearning for what resides

behind the eyes.

Pull me towards you —

you who makes the brew —

so I may sip the unseen

and her cascade of names.

So that even

after all the loneliness,

I am broken open

by the breath

of every infinite thing.

FOR CYNTHIA

Thought of you today

in the deep of my sleeve,

nestled between skin and cloth,

breathing so close to

my perseverant heart.

And I saw you today

as the crack in gray sky,

a beam of light, a match ignited

in the basement of night.

For you were not kind

because you had to be,

you were not good

because you were told,

you did not listen

just so you could speak.

Rather, you were of

the rarest of creatures

who gave just to give.

And still, in your absence,

you somehow gift us.

And still, in your absence,

you somehow arrive

from the train of memory

beaming with that thing

that goes beyond being alive.

And so if the dead

greet the dying,

I shall have

one single request

as I pass on:

will you envelop me

in your laughter,

wringing the fear out

of my scaling soul?

And together,

may we travel,

like a sudden silver wave

on the coastline of

the Atlantic shore,

crashing merrily on.

WILD WALTZ

When you lay to rest
the body I was birthed in,
I hope you say,
she was a wild waltz,
never crystallized by form
but a dance always being born.

THE SLEEVE FOR MY SOUL

Is my body that of bondage,
or is every cell a small sphere of divinity,
every vein a stream infused with spirit,
every wound a calling back home
to the heart and her maker?

For when I tire of trying to transcend,
I have you to nestle into —
the shape of which is the perfect
sleeve for my soul.

Tonight, I whisper thank you.
Tonight, I remember you are royal.

I REMEMBER NOW

Have you forgotten that your worth
is not tethered nor tied
to anything on the outside?

That you do not need to earn,
prove or beg for that
which is your birthright.

That just by being alive in this body,
you are a brilliant star
made of the one great mystery.

Let your bright flame burn.
Let your body dance in rivers.
Let the oceanic arms of love
cradle you into freedom.

Dear one,
place your precious hands
upon your own heart now.

These hands that are infused

with the arc of infinity.

This heart that blooms

with bountiful love.

And say,

I remember,

oh yes,

I remember now.

THE WORLD & I

I have seen dazzling lines of light
and called them shooting stars,
but I, a slight spectator,
cannot feel their blazing burn,
cannot see the chilling mesosphere
they so boldly enter, only to extinguish,
like kamikaze pilots who fly just to die.

And I have heard of a river running
in an Amazonian sky,
a river revealing itself in rain
to the jungle down below
where a green so grand glistens
and ceaseless sounds protest silence.

But I have tasted the red-ripened strawberry
and licked the juice of an orange peach
and I have looked to you
in ordinary evenings —
you in your lavender dress
with creamsicle clouds
and fading blue blush.

And I've called you my Earth,

called you my God,

called you my Sky,

as you flutter your wings

before surrendering

to another kind of life.

And though I will never

touch the star's flame,

never behold the river in the sky,

I know of a world

that paints and dances and drips.

I feel of a world

demanding to be alive.

And I,

a slight spectator,

and I.

GIFTS FROM THE MOUNTAINS

Come, dear one, and listen.
I do not care for speaking
nor hurrying about
from here to there.

Rather, will you sit with me
and sip in the world?
Will you steep your soul
in the sharing of silent rapture?

Will you travel, just before
the darkness relinquishes,
to see the sun rise like a halo?

Will you stop with me
and wrap your arms
around the ponderosa pine,
breathing in her butterscotch bark
and listen to the rustles
of a tiny chipmunk
buried in the bush?

Will you witness

the wings of the magpie

and her soft white belly

or the hawk circling above us

in search of his early morning feast?

Will you sink into the stone,

even when it is cold,

and let the vision

of the mountains warm you?

And will you leave behind

your stories of suffering,

if only for a short while,

to bask in the haven of

the untouched hills?

Will you call out to what is good

and what is holy

and to what was not made

by the hands of men?

And will you bring it back —

this peace and this rapture —

like a great bounty,

back to your cities and your homes,

emptying your hands

into the concrete streets.

And will you give,

just a little bit more,

of what the hills and the trees

and the sky have so selflessly

gifted to you,

scattering these pieces of beauty

like birdseed

amongst all the hardship.

CELEBRATION IS A BIRD

Celebration is a bird

inside my body —

her silver wings

threaded with gold

that flutter near

the face of my heart.

Open, she says

from her full brown beak,

to life.

Let the tide of the terrific

sweep you into remembrance.

All that is here —

every beauty, every ache,

every triumph, every joy —

is to be seen and celebrated.

Tie balloons around your burdens

and watch them float

towards the brushed blue sky.

Eat cake with the Beloved

and feel how a great joy

has found you and

greeted you as a friend.

All my life I have forgotten

this sweet freedom —

that froths at the mouth,

that tastes of honeysuckle

and sings in every cell.

All my life —

a celebration.

Every step —

a sonnet of birdsong.

THE ONE WHO WEAVES ME

In Honor of Rilke

What is the world
if not of your hands
weaving, always weaving,
a tapestry of tragedy
and transcendence?
Eternal Song, Silent One,
Divine Mother dancing
in my cheekbones —
oh please, serenade me.
Try, as I may,
to reach for you,
to clasp my fingers
through the seam of your skin.
Night after night, I weep
at the altar of your arrival.
I hear sirens, taste clouds,
watch children chase each other
in fields of bliss
and all I see are strings —
your strings —
bending, expanding, and knotting

into one another.

You see, what is the world

but a turning, always turning,

towards you the one who weaves me.

EPILOGUE

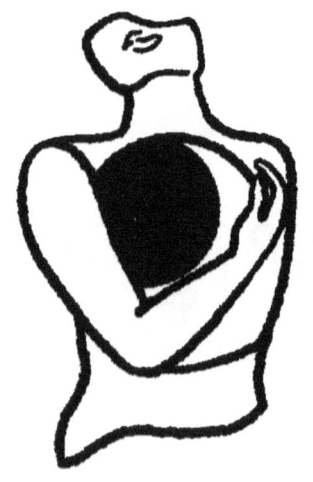

MEMENTO MORI

There will come a time when
all my seeking silences itself,
and I am left in a field
of primordial emptiness,

where every visitor will vanish
into the milky petals of the lily,
and the storms once so certain
will end in ceasefire,
reminding me
I was always awakened,

where after giving my body
so fully to this life,
I will crawl out of my chrysalis
and into the soft sky of stillness
with sacred wings
and a voice
finally free
to sing.

Acknowledgments

To my mama, I could not have done anything in my life without your love. Thank you for accepting every part of me. Thank you for giving me life. Thank you for listening to every poem, idea, and insight that traverses through my heart. You are my golden light.

To Dad and Sue, thank you for being my greatest cheerleaders. Thank you for seeing me in ways that I sometimes forget, for encouraging me always, and for supporting my dreams. You help me to remember who I am and for that I am forever grateful.

To Shannon, my beautiful sister, for every time you held my heart and my hand in moments of deep suffering, I thank you. For every time you inspired me to keep shining, I thank you. For every moment we have ever shared since we were little to now, I am so thankful.

To Kiki, my rainbow sister, thank you for being the first person to read every line of my manuscript. Thank you for encouraging me to share my voice with the world and for never letting me give up on my dreams. You will forever be my playmate. And to my other playmate, Cynthia, thank you for infusing your laughter and love into every ache and for teaching me that we never fully lose the ones we love.

To Brooke Sunderland, thank you for supporting my dreams and visions in a multitude of ways and for creating the beautiful art that graces this cover.

To my spirit family — Louis, Trinity, and Grace — thank you for teaching me what it means to be a spiritual warrior. Thank you for receiving my poems into the soft channels of your hearts and for sharing them in intimate and precious ways.

To Brooke McNamara and the Summoning the Unseen community, thank you for co-creating poetry and connection in a space devoted to being for each other. Many of these poems emerged from our shared space and beloved community. I bow in reverence to you all.

To Jana, my radiant one, you are a part of my heart. Thank you for meeting me in the waters of deep knowing, for celebrating every facet of my being, and for reflecting back to me my brilliance. It is an honor to dance beside you, even from across the world, on this incredible journey of life.

To my dear family, friends, mentors, teachers, and fellow poets, words would only fill a small cup of the love that I have for you. Thank you for being a part of this wild, messy and magical journey that is life.

Thank you to Spirit for breathing life into the world. May I continue to be a vessel of your love and a spark of your eternal flame.

And to the reader, thank you for reading my poems, these small snippets from my soul. May they serve as a reminder that you are never alone in this life, that you are a part of something greater — a love that will linger for eternity.

About Kailey

Kailey Murphy is a creative, sensitive soul devoted to supporting others in connecting with their bodies, unlocking their wisdom, and living their deepest devotion. She grew up in New York and now calls Boulder, Colorado home after many years of traveling and living in different communities around the world. Though she immersed herself in writing at a young age, her love for poetry blossomed after living with many creative beings at the Omega Institute. It was here that she tapped into a wellspring of words that rushed through her and onto the page. Over the years, Kailey has continued to deepen into this practice of writing by listening to her heart, by co-creating in community with other writers, and by learning the art of surrender. Kailey is also the creator of Moon Body Living, where she offers 1:1 embodiment coaching and guided meditations, rooted in somatic and spiritual exploration. *Between Me and My Bone*s is her first published book of poetry.

To learn more please visit:
www.moonbodyliving.com
IG @moonbodyliving